J. J. F. DOTZAUER

113 VIOLONCELLO-ETÜDEN
113 EXERCISES FOR VIOLONCELLO

Heft III
Nr. 63–85

Ausgewählt, progressiv geordnet und bezeichnet von
Selected, progressively arranged and fingered by

Johanns Klingenberg

ALLE RECHTE VORBEHALTEN · ALL RIGHTS RESERVED

EDITION PETERS
LEIPZIG · LONDON · NEW YORK

INHALT / CONTENTS

Cah. 4. (No. 86—113.)

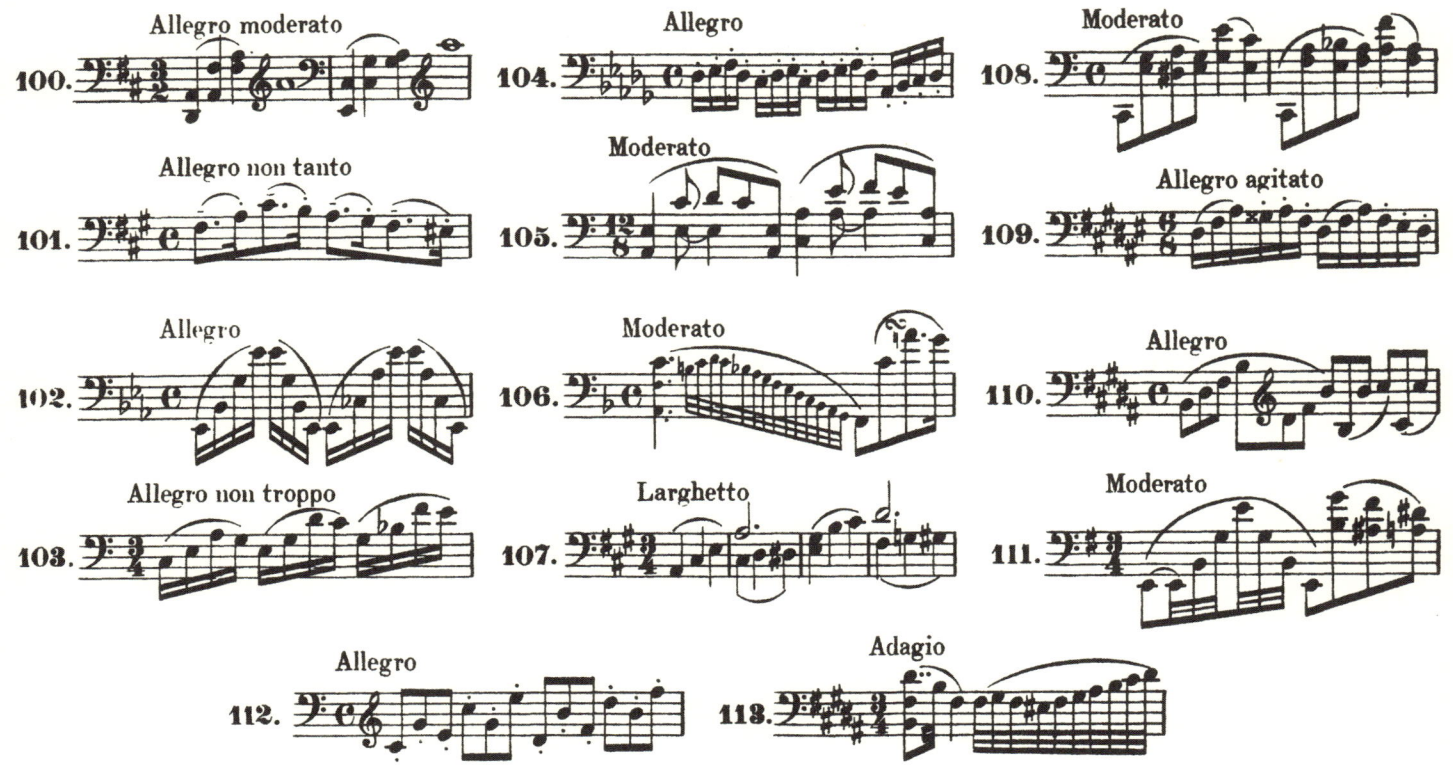

Zeichen und Abkürzungen
SIGNES ET ABRÉVIATIONS ✱ SIGNS AND ABBREVIATIONS

⊓	Herunterstrich.	⊓	Tirez.	⊓	Down bow.
V	Hinaufstrich	V	Poussez.	V	Up bow.
G.	Ganzer Bogen.	G.	Tout l'archet.	G.	Whole bow.
OH.	Oberer halber Bogen.	OH.	Moitié supérieure de l'archet.	OH.	Upper half of bow.
UH.	Unterer halber Bogen.	UH.	Moitié inférieure de l'archet.	UH.	Lower half of bow.
Fr.	Frosch des Bogens.	Fr.	Talon de l'archet.	Fr.	Nut of bow.
M.	Mitte des Bogens.	M.	Milieu de l'archet.	M.	Middle of bow.
Sp.	Spitze des Bogens.	Sp.	Pointe de l'archet.	Sp.	Point of bow.
⌐	Liegenlassen der Finger.	⌐	Laissez les doigts en place.	⌐	Keep the fingers in position.

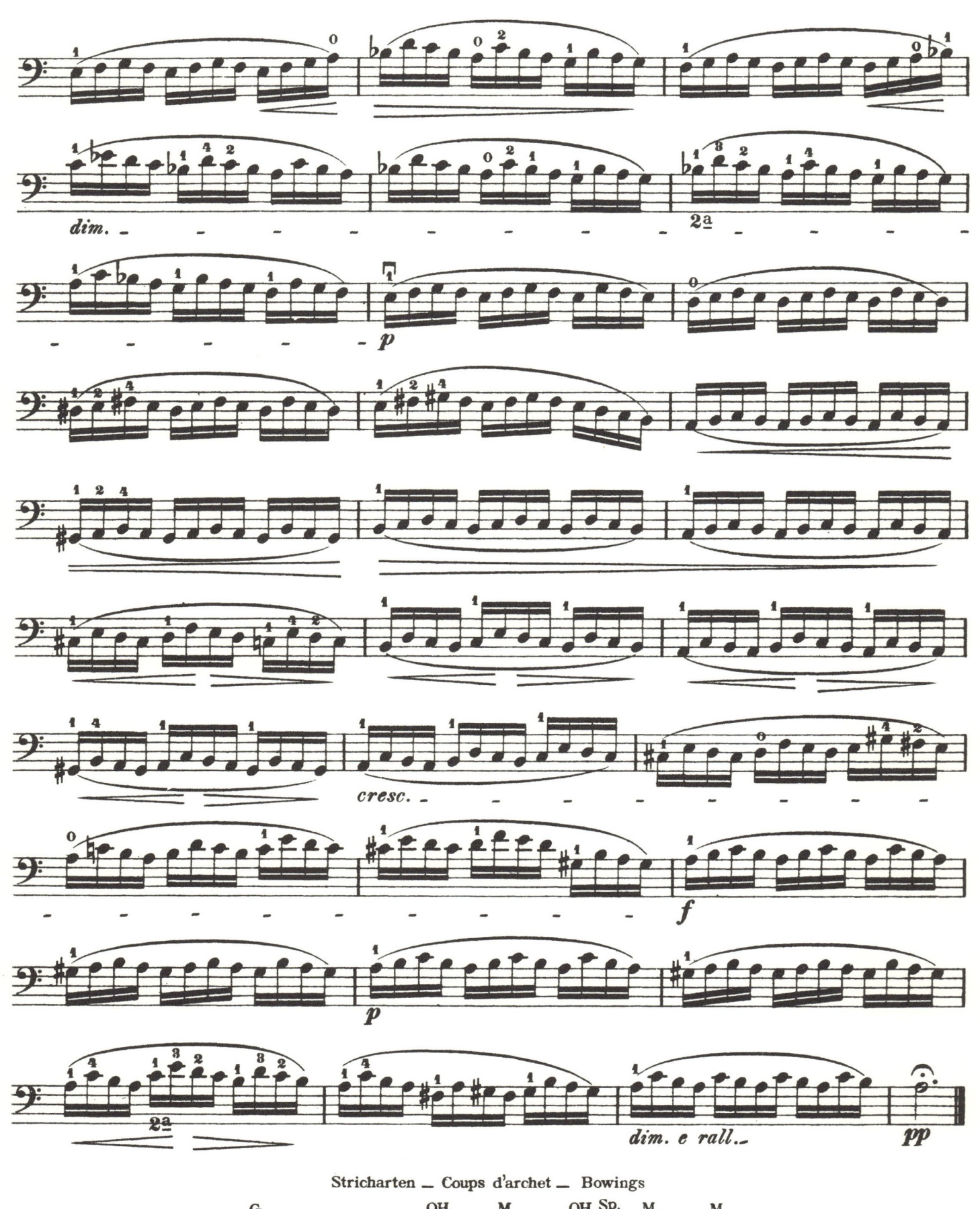

24

28

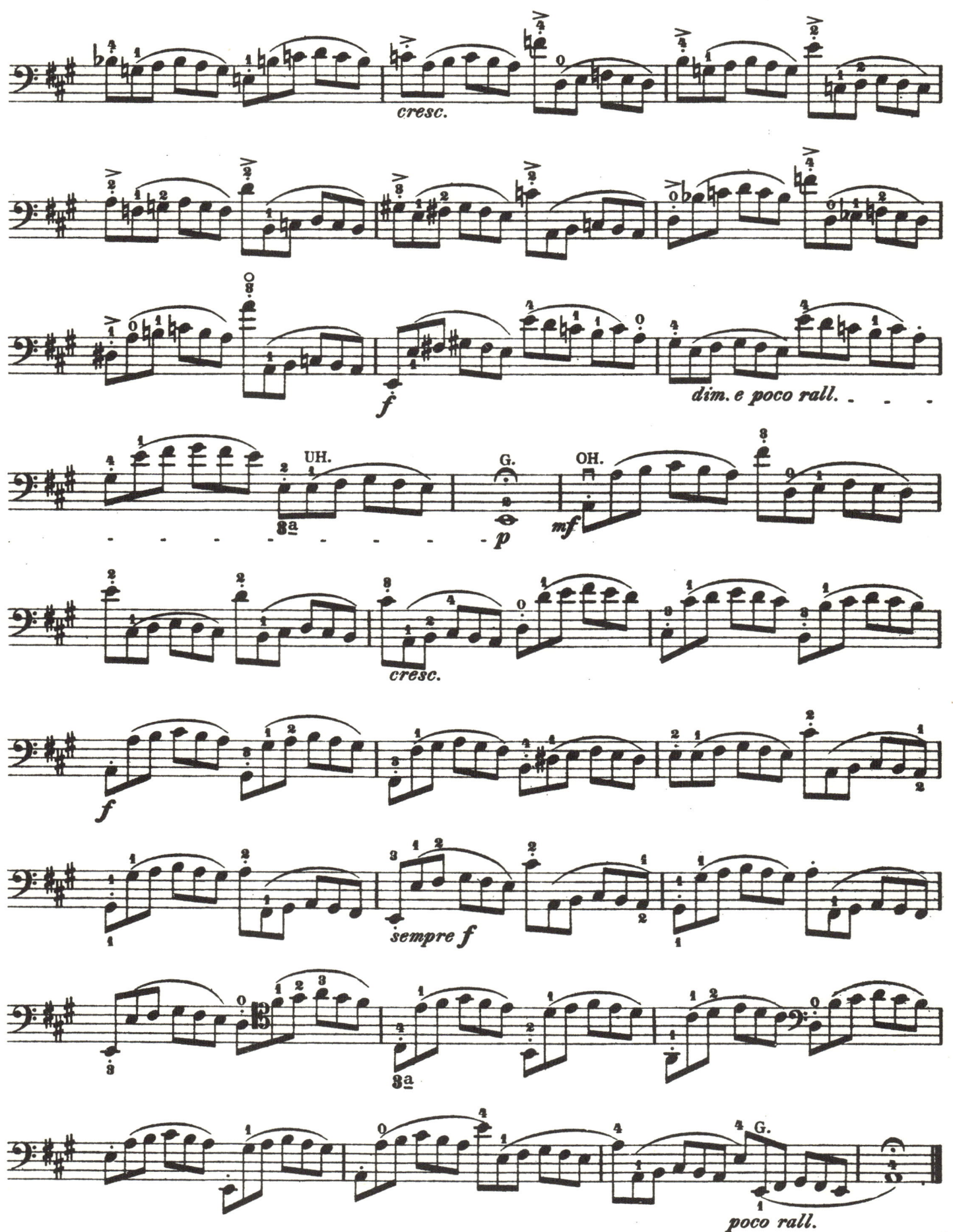

34

36

Stricharten — Coups d'archet — Bowings

30017

Durch alle Tonarten

Dans tous les tons majeurs et mineurs ✻ In all the major and minor keys

Allegro non troppo

85.

42